Doc Holliday Bat Masterson, & Wyatt Earp

Their Colorado Careers

By E. Richard Churchill

ISBN-13: 978-1-890437-64-0
ISBN-10: 1-890437-64-6

Published by:

WESTERN REFLECTIONS
PUBLISHING COMPANY
219 Main Street
Montrose, CO 81401
Email: westref@montrose.net
www.westernreflectionspub.com

Wyatt Earp

Denver Public Library, Western History Department

CHRONOLOGY

The lives of Doc Holliday, Bat Masterson, and Wyatt Earp were closely intertwined. They visited the same towns, lived similar lives, and on occasion fought the same battles. Oddly enough none of the three noted gunmen died by the gun, so even in death their lives were somewhat the same.

The following brief chronology is presented to aid the reader in relating their Colorado adventures with their exploits outside the borders of the Centennial State. Though the names Dodge City and Tombstone are perhaps better known as the stamping grounds of these three celebrated gun slingers, their travels took them in and out of Colorado on numerous occasions.

Wyatt Earp, born March 19, 1848, near Monmouth, Illinois.

John Henry "Doc" Holliday, born late January or early February, 1852, Griffin, Georgia.

William Barclay "Bat" Masterson, born 1855, on a farm in Iroquois County, Illinois.

December, 1869, Wyatt hired as a hunter for a party of surveyors leaving Springfield, Missouri.

1872, Doc graduated from Baltimore Dental School.

Winter of 1872-73, Bat and Wyatt meet on the Salt Fork of the Arkansas River. Both were professional hunters.

1873, Wyatt in Ellsworth, Kansas.

1874, Wyatt in Wichita, Kansas.

May 17, 1876, Wyatt reaches Dodge City, Kansas.

May or June, 1876, Doc leaves Texas and travels to Colorado.

Summer, 1876, Bat arrives in Dodge City.

November, 1877, Doc meets Wyatt in Forth Griffin, Texas.

November, 1877, Bat elected sheriff of Ford County, Kansas. (Dodge City.)

December, 1877, Doc goes to Dodge City.

1878, Wyatt returns to Dodge City.

1878-79, Royal Gorge Railroad War in Colorado involves Bat and Doc.

September 9, 1879, Wyatt leaves for Tombstone, Arizona.

February, 1880, Doc reaches Tombstone.

1881, Bat reaches Tombstone but returns to Dodge City, April 16, 1881.

Late April or early May, 1881, Bat becomes Trinidad, Colorado, peace officer.

October, 1881, Wyatt and Doc at O. K. Corral.

May 10, 1882, Wyatt and Doc reach Pueblo, Colorado, from Arizona.

May 15, 1882, Doc arrested in Denver, Colorado.

1882-83, Wyatt in Gunnison, Colorado, as gambler.

1882-87, Wyatt seen as gambler in Gunnison, Trinidad, Silverton, Aspen, and Denver, Colorado.

1883, Bat and Wyatt meet in Silverton, Colorado.

May, 1883, Doc visits Silverton, Colorado.

November, 1883, Doc moves to Leadville, Colorado.

August 19, 1884, Doc shoots Billy Allen in Leadville.

Mid 1880's, Bat living in Denver but touring Colorado mining camps as a gambler.

1885-87, Doc divides his time among Leadville, Denver, and Pueblo.

May, 1887, Doc moves to Glenwood Springs, Colorado.

November 8, 1887, Doc dies at Glenwood Springs.

1892, Bat follows mining boom to Creede, Colorado.

1897, Wyatt in Nome, Alaska.

1899, Bat becomes Denver fight promoter.

September, 1900, Bat leaves Colorado for the East.

October 25, 1921, Bat dies at desk in New York City.

January 13, 1929, Wyatt dies in Los Angeles, California.

John Henry "Doc" Holliday

Denver Public Library, Western History Department

4

ENTER DOC HOLLIDAY

Colorado lacked months of acquiring statehood when the slightly built, well-dresser gambler first viewed Pueblo, Colorado. His flight from Texas had been both swift and necessary. A fast gun quite often required a fast exit. In an effort to make his Colorado sojourn pleasant Doc Holliday had taken a new name. He greeted Pueblo as Tom McKey (McKee).

A brief glance was all the celebrated John Henry Holliday gave Pueblo before moving on to Denver. There he set about establishing himself as Tom McKey, gambler. Doc of the competent hands and cool nerve found ready employment as a faro dealer for Charley Foster who ran Babbitt's House at 357 Blake Street. When Doc wasn't working his eight hour shift at Babbitt's he was more likely than not to be found gambling in one of the many available places along either Blake or Larimer Streets. Big Ed Chase's place was a frequent stopping point for the dentist-turned gambler.

Doc, like others possessed of his adventuring spirit, took a number of jaunts to various of Colorado's mining camps. Central City, Black Hawk, Idaho Springs, Georgetown, Rosita, and Boulder all hosted him during the summer of 1876. Several reports of gun-play during his tour are rumored though history fails to record names and dates of fatalities, if any.

That fall Doc visited Deadwood, stopping on the way at Cheyenne. Neither place seemed to appeal greatly to him so Doc, still as Tom McKey, returned to Babbitt's faro table in Denver. Doc's use of the McKey name had been intended to keep him out of trouble. However, his well-intentioned name change may have had the opposite effect, at least in one instance.

Bat Masterson later recounted that instance as one of Doc's more violent Denver adventures during this period in his life. Local custom forbade the carrying of firearms in the capital city of the nation's newest state. However, this rule seemed to have been enforced only insofar as outsiders were concerned. The local lads seem to have been allowed to ignore the rule without serious consequences. The slightly built Doc who was never in good health felt he need of some sort of equalizer as he plied his trade. To make up for the lack of a Colt he took to carrying a well sharpened knife concealed but readily accessible should circumstances demand its use.

One Bud (Budd) Ryan took exception to Doc's card playing. Had Bud known the faro dealer was Doc Holliday he might well have kept his problem to himself. Thin, coughing Tom McKey was entirely a different matter. Blustering Bud made vocal threats and began the process of producing his revolver to further intimidate the slight, dark-haired gambler across the table from him.

While Ryan unlimbered his weapon Holliday, having decided the situation warranted such action, produced his well-honed blade and, like a cat, was upon Ryan before the larger man was fully aware of the change in plan. According to Masterson, Doc's impromptu surgery took the fight out of Ryan while serving as a teachable moment for other members of Denver's gambling fraternity. A doctor made the necessary repairs to Bud's throat and Doc finished out the season without further recorded conflict.

The following summer Doc broadened his activities to include those of confidence man. His scheme was far from original but P. T. Barnum knew of what he spoke. Suckers appeared if not every minute, at least often enough to keep Doc and his accomplices busy.

Doc took to riding the Union Pacific with a gold-plated brick of lead as his primary luggage. It was not difficult for Doc, a well-educated Southerner, to pass himself off on the unsuspecting as a mine owner, or engineer, or what have you. From that point it took no real effort for Doc to let his victim know he, Doc, had a gold brick for sale at a bargain price. Perhaps it was stolen; perhaps merely mislaid. It didn't matter. Once Doc had the full attention of a well-heeled sucker one thing was certain. Doc would shortly be holding his victim's cash and the victim would be left holding a handsomely gilded leaden brick.

But not for long. Scarcely had Doc left the train before a pair of grim-faced, hard-eyed "Pinkertons" confronted the proud possessor of the gilded brick. Seems the brick was sure enough stolen. Guess who was now in possession of stolen property. Somehow the sucker was always able to convince the "Pinkertons" that he was actually a victim, not the perpetrator of the theft. Usually a substantial payment of cash helped the "Pinkertons" forget the whole thing so long as the brick was recovered.

Immediately upon recovering the brick the "Pinkertons" left the train to rejoin Doc. The sucker continued his journey much poorer but possibly wiser, no doubt feeling himself lucky to still be aboard the train rather than in jail. Should a victim of Doc's con tumble to the fact he had been taken not once but twice he was still out of luck. His only evidence, the leaden brick, was long since out of his hands. Not only did this protect Doc but it cut down on his overhead as well.

Meanwhile Doc, brick, and friends were reunited and in search of another traveler who might like to acquire a gold brick — cheap.

Royal Gorge Warriors — Bat and Doc

While Bat, Doc and Wyatt were becoming better acquainted in Dodge City, a pair of Colorado railroads were literally at the throats of one another. The Denver and Rio Grande could not seem to agree with the Atchison, Topeka and Santa Fe concerning which road was to use which right of way and consequently serve which areas.

The conflict centered on Raton Pass between Trinidad, Colorado, and Las Vegas, New Mexico, and the Royal Gorge through which the Arkansas River had carved a path on its way to the Gulf. On April 10, 1878, the Santa Fe had announced it intended to build a line through the Royal Gorge. Its destination was silver-rich Leadville, Colorado. General William J. Palmer, head of the Denver and Rio Grande, took exception to the Santa Fe's plans. Palmer's crews at once began building their own line into the narrow defile.

The two warring factions drew immediate battle lines. While opposing attorneys prepared to do battle in court, crews from both roads prepared to do battle on a more personal level. One of the first steps for both roads was the construction of stone forts overlooking the depths of the Royal Gorge at strategic points. The state's newspapers joined in the fray. The **Rocky Mountain News** favored the Rio Grande while the Denver **Tribune** gave its best for the Santa Fe. Other papers divided their support between the two rail companies.

The stage was set for Colorado's first real railroad war. News releases added to the drama of the moment. It seemed certain blood would flow track deep before the final decision was reached. As both sides gathered arms and ammunition the Santa Fe decided to leave nothing to chance. A recruiter was dispatched to Dodge City where one John Joshua Webb was picked to lead a detachment of mercenaries into Colorado. Bat

Forts in the Royal Gorge

Denver Public Library, Western History Department

found time to leave his lawman duties and Doc his faro table. Another dozen and a half gunmen of lesser stature swelled the ranks.

Eddie Foy was performing in Dodge City at the time. He records the fact that Doc tried to recruit him for the venture. Foy declined due to lack of skill and, perhaps, lack of love of that sort of adventure. Foy recorded Doc's reply, "Oh, that's all right. The Santy Fee won't know the difference. You kin use a shotgun if you want to. Dodge wants to make a good showin' in this business. You'll help swell the crowd, and you'll get your pay anyhow." Even so Foy stood firm. When the Dodge City detachment left for Colorado Foy was not among them.

While Bat and Doc and the others rode in wagons into the depths of the Royal Gorge to guard a surveying party, the legal heads of both roads met in court. The first round went to the Santa Fe by unanimous decision. As a result of the court's ruling the Rio Grande was forced to turn over miles of track and accompanying depots to the Santa Fe on a thirty year lease. From that point things indeed became lively.

William B. Strong of the Santa Fe took five hundred riflemen with him and ensured that strategic Raton Pass was in the proper hands, at least from his point of view. A number of Santa Fe rail agents shortly found themselves captives of the opposition. Rio Grande work parties were sniped at. A court decision handed down in early 1879 gave **both** lines the right to use the Gorge. This only complicated matters due to the fact there simply was not room for two tracks to run side by side through many points in the thousand foot deep canyon.

In June the situation came to a head in the Roundhouse Battle at Pueblo. The Santa Fe, having gotten word that General Palmer was preparing an invasion force, had chosen the roundhouse as its defense line. Bat and perhaps fifty gunmen had fortified the roundhouse. In addition to their normal collection of rifles, revolvers, and shotguns, the Santa Fe men had acquired a gatling gun. Perhaps even more lethal was Bat's recent appointment as a United States deputy marshal. Santa

William Jackson Palmer

Denver Public Library, Western History Department

Fe's political influence had gotten the appointment so Bat could "legally" defend Santa Fe property.

A Rio Grande special fast approached the roundhouse. Aboard the screaming special were several hundred armed men led by General Palmer. Also aboard was Robert F. Weitbrec, treasurer for the Rio Grande. Weitbrec's only armament consisted of a satchel he held in a firm grasp. When the special ground to a halt Palmer immediately deployed his forces around the roundhouse. Inside the building Bat and his gunmen braced for the attack.

Before blood was spilled Weitbrec and his satchel approached the roundhouse under a flag of truce. Bat left the fortress and walked out to meet the Rio Grande emissary. The two conferred for the better part of an hour. Then both bowed in a formal manner and parted. The satchel was lighter and Bat's pockets fuller as the two men returned to their forces. Bat's staunch defenders divided the ten thousand dollar bribe and surrendered the strong point without a shot.

Actually, the joke was on the Rio Grande. Bat had been notified the roundhouse was no longer essential to Santa Fe defenses. Santa Fe held Raton Pass secure and the courts were to work out the Royal Gorge situation without violence. The Great Royal Gorge War and Roundhouse Battle had both ended with neither Bat nor Doc firing a shot in anger.

While Bat hurried back to his neglected duties at Dodge City where he served as Ford County's Sheriff, Doc turned to Trinidad's gambling halls for a bit of relaxation. Shortly, a gambler named Kid Colton ran afoul of Doc and was shot for his efforts. The Kid survived but Doc felt June a good time to swing down to Las Vegas, New Mexico, for a bit of gambling and, incidentally, another shooting.

The Gallows Beckon to Doc in Denver

In the spring of 1881, Bat moved to Trinidad, Colorado, where he found ready employment as both peace officer and gambler. The combination was a common one during the day. A noted gunslinger was an asset to any gambling establishment and, in the event of trouble, the law was already at hand. Thus, while Doc and the Earps were throwing lead at the O. K. Corral, Bat was enjoying Colorful Colorado.

On May 10, 1882, Doc and Wyatt Earp reached Pueblo, Colorado. The Eastern Slope of the Rockies was still to Doc's liking. He decided to again try his luck in the area, though this time as Doc Holliday, not as Tom McKey. Evidently he and Wyatt disagreed. Wyatt was fearful of the situation so recently behind them in Arizona. He elected to travel on to Gunnison, Colorado, leaving Doc to his own devices.

While in Pueblo Doc had a strange encounter. A total stranger accosted Doc in Tom Kemp's variety theater and proceeded to thank Doc for having saved his life in Santa Fe. As repayment he wanted to do a favor for Doc. Doc told the man favors were welcome but in this case undeserved as he had not saved the man's life in Santa Fe or anywhere else. Doc's admission notwithstanding the stranger informed Doc he had just come up on the train. Aboard the train was Josh Stilwell. Josh, he told Doc, was gunning for Holliday to avenge the killing of his brother Frank Stilwell who Wyatt had dealt with in Tucson.

Doc was neither surprised nor concerned at the information. He was a bit taken aback when the other peeled off his clothing to display a "bullet wound" as some sort of proof or other. Doc recognized the mark as being far removed from a bullet wound, laughed at the man and dismissed the matter from his mind.

The following Sunday, May 14, Doc decided to travel to Denver to take in the races at the Fair Ground the following Tuesday. Doc missed the races, though by the time they were run he had other things on his mind.

Monday, as Doc walked a Denver street, he was suddenly confronted by two drawn revolvers and the command, "Throw up your hands." The guns were held by none other than the man he had met in Pueblo a few days previously. In the company of Arapahoe County sheriff's deputies Charles T. Linton and Barney Cutler, Doc was hustled off to the sheriff's office. There he found his informant-turned-captor was called Perry M. Mallen.

Mallen, so he said, was a deputy sheriff from Los Angeles. He had hunted Doc for seven years for the killing of his partner, one Harry White. The killing, which occurred in Utah, had started Mallen on a series of adventures and near encounters with death as he relentlessly stalked Doc. The fact that Doc had never been in Utah, much less killed one Harry White, made little difference at that moment. A noted gunman was in custody and Sheriff Michael Spangler meant to keep him.

The events which followed set in motion a fantastic legal and newspaper feud from which the bad guy (Doc) emerged the good guy and the good guys (Mallen, et al) emerged with egg completely covering their faces.

Mallen accused Doc of crimes almost too numerous to mention among which were accessory to the murder of Frank Stilwell in Tucson, murder of a railway conductor, murder of a rancher, and on and on ad nauseam. Doc tried to address the growing crowd assembled in the sheriff's office but was cut short in his efforts by Mallen and a deputy. A **Tribune** reporter described the gambler as cool; Mallen as excited. When the initial excitement abated somewhat Doc was moved to the Arapahoe County jail. His one request was for Bat Masterson.

The relationship between Bat and Doc was curiously dependent upon the relationship of both with Wyatt Earp. In response to Doc's plea and a later telegram from Wyatt, Bat traveled post haste to Denver. There he told a **Republican** reporter, "I tell you this talk about Holliday is wrong. I know him well. He was with me in Dodge, where he was known as an enemy of the lawless element." Bat further charged that Mallen was a fraud. Later he made the same charge to Mallen's face. Mallen wisely refrained from calling Bat a liar. When the **Tribune** called Bat the "man who smiles" they didn't mean his smile meant humor. Obviously Mallen had realized this to be the case.

Even though Bat publicly supported Doc and worked actively for Doc's release, he really had little love for the deadly Doc. Stuart Lake later reported the following view of Doc as seen by Bat. "Doc had few real friends," Bat Masterson said.

"He was selfish and of a perverse nature, characteristics not calculated to make a man popular on the frontier. I never liked Holliday; I tolerated him and helped him at times solely on Wyatt Earp's account, as did many others. As far as I can recall, Doc had but three redeeming traits. One was his courage; he was afraid of nothing on earth. The second was the one commendable principle in his code of life, sterling loyalty to friends. The third was his affection for Wyatt Earp. The depth of this sentiment was shown not only by Doc's demonstrated willingness to stake his life for Wyatt without second thought; it was even more clearly established by the fact that, despite his almost uncontrollable temper and his maniacal love of a fight, Doc Holliday could avoid trouble when there was a possibility that some encounter might prove embarassing to Wyatt. On more than one occasion Doc actually backed down before men whom he easily could have killed, simply because gunplay at the time would have reacted unfavorably against Wyatt. To appreciate that fully, you had to know Holliday."

Bat's personal regard for Wyatt far outweighed his lack of love for Doc. Doc needed help and Bat was able to provide that help. The Trinidad peace officer wasn't alone, however. Two Denver papers, the **Tribune** and the **Republican,** began to champion Doc's cause as did Pueblo's **Chieftain.**

The **Chieftain** was quick to spot Mallen for what he was — a reward seeking imposter. A quick review of Mallen's brief stay in Pueblo revealed he was most probably from Akron, Ohio. While in Pueblo he had managed to secure money from other Ohio natives; money he neglected to return when he departed for Denver. In addition he had borrowed ten dollars from a bartender. This likewise remained unpaid. Further, it seems the good Mallen had represented himself varyingly as a government detective and a United States Marshal during his brief but busy Pueblo sojourn.

In conclusion the **Chieftain** described Mallen as a "small man, with reddish face and beard, with small ferretty eyes, and not an inviting cast of features." Doc, on the other hand, "is a man of light weight, rather tall, smoothly shaven, and is always well dressed. Streaks of grey can be seen in his hair . . . His eyes are blue, large, sharp and piercing." It wasn't hard to tell where the **Chieftain's** sympathies lay.

The **Rocky Mountain News** saw things differently. Editor W. N. Byers hated the outlaw element. His paper was vocal in its demands that Doc meet justice. The intrigue surrounding the case, however, was more than even the **News** could handle as the plot unfolded.

Sheriff Spangler wired Arizona's Governor F. A. Tritle. The good sheriff told Tritle Doc **and** the Earps were in custody. What did the governor desire? What indeed? A telegram from Sheriff Byres of Gunnison followed quickly. Did Arizona authorities wish for him to arrest Wyatt Earp who was then in Gunnison? Sheriff Johnny Behan denounced Byres as a fraud and made ready to pick up his old enemies. Governor Tritle had other plans. He sent Sheriff Bob Paul of Pima County to Denver. It seems Governor Tritle trusted Behan no further than did Doc.

Doc was meanwhile telling a reporter from the Denver **Republican,** "If I am taken back to Arizona, that is the last of Holliday." He further charged that Behan was in close association with the Rustlers and himself a criminal. Of Sheriff Bob Paul Doc said, "He is a good man, but I am afraid he cannot protect me. The jail is a little tumble-down affair, which a few men can push over, and a few cans of oil thrown upon it would cause it to burn up in a flash, and either burn a prisoner to death or drive him out to be shot down. That will be my fate."

The **News** countered with comments from an unidentified gentleman "from Arizona" who claimed Virgil Earp had once bunced a man in Tombstone. It naturally followed that Doc was guilty of murder in Tucson, or so the **News** reasoned.

While Doc talked to reporters and Sheriff Paul gathered extradition papers, Bat was doing his own bit on Doc's behalf. Attorneys Frank Naylor and Colonel John T. Deweese had persuaded Judge Victor A. Elliott to sign a writ of habeas corpus. Bat, as Las Animas County deputy sheriff, had filed charges against Doc as operator of a confidence game in which one hundred and fifty dollars had been taken. City Marshal Jamieson issued a warrant for Doc's arrest at Bat's request.

Bat's strategy was simple but sound. If the habeas corpus writ could be used to free Doc from Mallen's flimsy charges before Bob Paul arrived with extradition papers, the battle would be half over. Doc could then be immediately arrested for the alleged bunco charge in Pueblo. Once in Bat's custody Doc could be held indefinitely in southern Colorado no matter how many extradition papers were served from Arizona.

Things went according to plan to a point. Doc's attorneys Naylor and Deweese, aided by the firm of Deckard and Yonley, secured a hearing before Judge Elliott on May 22 and 23. The judge discharged Doc. Instantly Deputy Sheriff Charles T. Linton of Arapahoe County presented a warrant for Doc's arrest for the murder of Frank Stilwell. The hearing was set for Friday, May 26.

Sheriff Paul arrived with extradition papers. The **News** crowed happily. But all was not lost. Governor Frederick W. Pitkin was "absent" from the city until Monday. Accordingly the extradition hearing was set for May 30. On the evening of Monday, May 29, E. D. Cowen of the **Tribune** paid Governor Pitkin a visit at Bat's request. Masterson felt Doc's life was endangered. Newsman Cowen had been convinced to plead Doc's case before the governor.

The following day Governor Pitkin appeared in court to say the extradition papers were improperly drawn and could not be honored. "In the second place it was the custom in cases where the person charged with an offense in one State was arrested for another offense in the State in which he lived the trial of the offense committed in the State in which he lived must precede his delivery to the authorities of the other State."

In other words Bat's phony charge took precedence over the murder charge which was, of course, also phony. Bat promptly arrested Doc and hustled him off to Pueblo that evening. Bob Paul returned to Arizona but in view of the good things he had said to reporters about Doc one is led to suspect Sheriff Paul was pleased to return home without Doc. Only the **News** was unhappy. Its unhappiness was to grow, however.

On Wednesday, May 31, Doc appeared before Justice McBride in Pueblo. The charge was swindling. Doc paid three

Frederick W. Pitkin

Denver Public Library, Western History Department

hundred dollars bail and his case was bound over for District Court. Doc promptly settled down as a gambler in South Pueblo where he was something of a tourist attraction. On July 18, 1882, he was charged with larceny but the case was continued.

Back to the **News,** however. On Friday, June 2, the **Republican** had the last word in the running feud which had centered on Doc and Perry Mallen. The **Republican** had picked up an item from the Cincinnati **Enquirer** datelined Denver, May 23, 1882. Gleefully the **Republican** recounted the fantastic tale which had Mallen being shot six times by Doc over a period of seven years. Additionally Doc had knifed the poor man as well. During one two week period in Tucson Doc had killed six men, bringing his career total to about fifty. The **Republican's** reporter was delighted but his delight was to grow when he discovered that Mallen had departed from Denver. Before leaving he had managed to "borrow" one hundred sixty-one dollars and a revolver from two Denver men. The funds were to help finance Mallen's "search" for a "wanted" man in Kansas City. Somehow Mallen and money had gone down the road together.

Much later Mallen was arrested in Pittsburgh but his Denver saga was at an end.

Unanswered questions remained unanswered to this day. For starters, who was Perry Mallen? Was he a bungling reward hunter or merely an unpolished con man? Did Arizona's Governor Tritle deliberately send improperly drawn extradition papers to Colorado? Was it just luck that Colorado's Governor Pitkin was out of town when the extradition papers arrived? Had the two governors previously agreed upon Colorado as a sanctuary for Doc and Wyatt?

Doc's Last Bow

While Doc and Bat struggled on the Eastern Slope of the Rockies Wyatt had crossed the Continental Divide to Gunnison. There he camped for a time with friends along the Gunnison River near Chinery Ranch. It was his intention to remain in Gunnison until his Arizona difficulties had abated somewhat.

Wyatt evidently found Gunnison to his liking for he stayed on through the winter of 1882-83. He was quick to find a job

Gunnison Colorado's Virginia Avenue

Denver Public Library, Western History Department

19

running a faro bank. The faro layout was situated on the second floor of the building which housed the barber shop and saloon owned by Ernest F. Bieble on Virginia Avenue, west of Main Street. According to contemporary accounts Wyatt was a "fine looking man" with drooping mustaches, who, while in Gunnison, caused no trouble. Though Wyatt told the police he was available if needed the need seems never to have materialized. The two revolvers he wore high under his arms were never drawn in anger in Gunnison.

Shortly after Wyatt's arrival the gunman was pointed out to a reporter who described him as a "rather tall, well dressed, pleasant looking stranger who stood leaning against the counter, tapping his boot with his cane." In the interview which followed Wyatt told the reporter, "I shall stay here for awhile. My lawyers will have a petition for my pardon drawn up. We look for a pardon in a few weeks, and when it comes I'll go back [to Tombstone]; but if no pardon is made I'll go back in the fall anyway and stand trial."

Fall came and went and Wyatt did not return to Tombstone, choosing instead to accept the hospitality offered by Gunnison. It is said that Doc camped with Wyatt for a time and on occasion drank too much. It seems unlikely that Doc ever saw Wyatt after they separated in Pueblo in May of 1882.

During the next five years Wyatt was in and out of Colorado's mining camps and boom towns as a gambler, though never as a peace officer. Both he and Bat met in Silverton in 1883, evidently missing Doc who arrived there in May. Wyatt dealt faro in both Trinidad and Denver, working down the street from Bat in Denver for a time. Aspen also beckoned to Wyatt at the time Doc was just over Independence Pass in Leadville.

By November, 1883, Doc had taken up somewhat permanent residence in two-mile high Leadville, dubbed Cloud City with a good cause. Doc's health was steadily failing and he suffered in Leadville which is noted for "having ten months of winter and two of mighty late fall." However, Leadville had miners. Miners liked to gamble. Doc gambled to live, therefore Leadville became Doc's home.

A Leadville, Colorado, Saloon

Denver Public Library, Western History Department

21

Doc moved into upstairs rooms above 106 East Second and at once began dealing faro at the Monarch Saloon on Harrison Avenue where owner Cy Allen knew a good thing when he saw it. At the nearby Casino worked a dealer named John Tyler. A few years previously Doc had backed Wyatt Earp when Earp bodily threw Tyler from the Oriental Saloon in Tombstone. Doc made a point of meeting Tyler openly but Tyler declined the opportunity of offering a challenge he might well regret.

While Doc settled down to his faro dealing Tyler began to campaign behind the tubercular gambler's back. Tyler's constant stirring of trouble paid dividends at last. One of his buddies picked a fight with Doc. Doc won the battle but lost the war. Cy Allen fired Doc as a troublemaker.

Broke, without a job, Doc's troubles were added to by a bout with pneumonia. He moved to a rent-free room above Manie Hyman's saloon on Harrison Avenue and managed to exist. A friendly bartender at the Monarch loaned Doc five dollars to tide him over. The bartender was one-time police chief Billy Allen. Unknown to Doc was the fact that Billy Allen was one of Tyler's numerous side kicks.

Doc meanwhile had recovered from his pneumonia to the extent he was able to begin dealing faro in Hyman's saloon. Weakened as he was by the combination of pneumonia and tuberculosis, the emaciated Doc presented anything but a threatening figure. When the down-on-his-luck gambler failed to repay the five dollar loan Billy Allen began to make public boasts that Doc would pay or be whipped. Billy finally set Tuesday, August 19, 1884, as the date by which Doc would make payment or suffer the consequences. Doc asked his one-time benefactor E. D. Cowen to witness the affair on his behalf. Cowen was then reporting for the Leadville **Democrat** and a capable witness.

Doubtless the urgings of Tyler had given Allen confidence. Also contributing to his boldness was the fact that Doc then weighed a mere 122 pounds compared to Allen's 170. The knowledge that Doc no longer wore a gun probably gave courage to Allen as well.

22

Leadville, Colorado

State Historical Society of Colorado Library

When Allen blustered through the swinging doors of Hyman's saloon Doc was standing behind a cigar case at the end of the bar. Doc's hand dropped below the counter to pick up a short barrelled Colt a friend had previously placed there for Doc's use. Within seconds Doc had separated the men from the boys as it were. Doc's first shot missed its mark and lodged in the door frame. Allen panicked and stumbled. Doc's second shot hit the fallen Allen in his gun arm. A bystander kept Doc from firing a third shot at the frantically retreating Allen who had just experienced more gun play than he really wanted.

While Allen was carted away for treatment, police captain Bradbury disarmed Doc and escorted him to jail. Doc's only request was that Bradbury keep him from being shot in the back. A week later Bradbury testified in court that he had warned Allen against entering Hyman's that day. Several witnesses testified to having heard Allen threaten to whip Doc. Judge Old set bail at eight thousand dollars which was produced by Leadville citizens. Doc went back to the gambling scene, something of a public figure, while he awaited his trial which was set for the coming spring.

All too often an individual refuses to let the law take its course. Such was the case of Constable Kelly. Kelly set out to avenge the shooting of Allen. He made the rounds of the saloons looking for Doc. Unfortunately for Kelly his search was successful. Doc asked whether the vengeful Kelly was armed. Kelly went for his weapon in reply. Doc's answer was in the same vein. Kelly was carried away to die and Doc was arrested once more, though more as a formality since Doc had acted in self defense.

Doc came to trial for shooting Allen on March 28, 1885. Colonel Deweese had journeyed up from Denver to act in Doc's defense. The court acquitted Doc on March 30. It was, in a sense, a victory of sorts for Allen. Never before had Doc been brought to trial for a shooting. Following the court's ruling, officers escorted Doc to catch the evening train out of Leadville to Colorado Springs and Denver.

Upon reaching Denver Doc checked in at the Metropolitan Hotel on Sixteenth Street. Between April, 1885, and May, 1887,

Doc gambled in Denver, Pueblo, and finally Leadville. On August 3, 1886, he was arrested for vagrancy in Denver. His case was continued, indefinitely it seems. Doc continued to divide his time among Denver, Pueblo, and Leadville while his health worsened daily.

In May, 1887, Doc decided to play for his biggest stake. He boarded a stage at Carson's stage and express line in Leadville. When the coach pulled away from the building on West Fourth it carried Doc toward Glenwood Springs where the sulfur baths were reported to work wonders. The famous mineral baths failed to arrest Doc's tuberculosis.

Shortly before 10:00 a. m. Tuesday, November 8, 1887, Doc drank a glass of whiskey. He lay back on his bed and said, "This is funny." A few minutes later John Henry Holliday was dead. "This is funny," was in reference to the fact a bullet had not gotten him despite his predictions that such would be the case.

That afternoon Doc was buried at Linwood Cemetery, bringing a close to the life, though not the legend, of Doc Holliday.

Bat's Years as a Sporting Man

Bat, like Wyatt, managed to keep his six-gun holstered in Colorado. Despite fanciful accounts to the contrary, Bat was not a hardened killer. Rather than the much distorted two dozen and more killings credited to him, Bat's true kill record could be counted on the fingers of one hand. His Colorado career during the late 1880's and 1890's bears out his basically calm nature.

This is not to say that Bat didn't have his share of adventures during those fifteen years. For instance there was the time when Bat "eloped" with the wife of comedian Louis Spencer. That was September 21, 1886. According to Spencer, "The trouble commenced Saturday night. I saw my wife sitting on Bat Masterson's knee in a box during the performance. I went to the door and called her out, and asked her what she was doing. Masterson spoke up and said that if I had anything to say to the lady I might tell it to him. I reminded him that the lady was my wife, when he struck at me with his pistol, and I struck back with my fist. Then we were arrested and taken down to the station, where we were both released . . . "

William Barclay "Bat" Masterson

State Historical Society of Colorado Library

26

The **Rocky Mountain News** reported that Bat and Mrs. Spencer were en route to Dodge City and summarized the situation with, "W. B. Masterson is well known in this city. He is a handsome man, and one who pleases the ladies." Nothing more was heard of the adventure and Bat shortly returned to Denver sans the lovely lady.

The paths of Bat and Wyatt had crossed and recrossed throughout the early and mid 1880's. Their final major crossing came in Denver. At the time Bat was dealing faro at the Arcade, Wyatt was at the nearby Central doing the same chore for gamblers Ed Chase and Ed Gaylord. The two, Bat and Wyatt, shared the same boarding house where their quick-draw practice did little to soothe the nerves of their fellow boarders.

By the close of the 1880's Bat had all but forsaken the life of the gun slinging lawman in favor of more peaceful pursuits. Though Bat numbered among his friends such characters as underworld czar Lou Blonger and his huge, but stupid brother Sam, Bat's gun was not for hire save as a peace keeping device where he was employed.

Employment for Bat most often centered around gambling and the world of the gambler. One of the gambling tales told of Bat involved a late night faro game with John Hapenny in Denver. During the game Bat began telling a Leadville tale. Hapenny became so absorbed in the story he left the cards in piles just as they had been played. Mechanically he replaced the cards in the box without so much as even a mention of a shuffle. When some newcomers arrived John began to deal the unshuffled cards. Bat had a tab giving the last deal and was quick to take advantage of the situation. Using his record Bat was soon several hundred dollars ahead as Hapenny pondered and worried. Before Bat cleaned him, Hapenny closed up shop for the night. It was several months later that Hapenny was finally told what had happened to him.

Bat's sense of humor appeared in other places than at the faro table with poor John Hapenny. By 1891 Bat had pretty much made Denver his home. For a time he managed a burlesque troupe at the Palace Theater. During Bat's stay at the

28

Palace he established a set of rules among which were the following:

> "Performers writing to this house for an engagement will state . . . the amount of salary they will work for, not what they want, for we make all the allowances for a performer's gall."

> "Variety ladies with more than three husbands need not write to this house for a date."

On November 21, 1891, Bat married Emma Walters, one of the Palace dancers, who remained his wife until death parted them nearly thirty years later.

Shortly after his wedding the lure of adventure once more cried out to Bat. The roaring mining camp called Creede beckoned enticingly. There Bat was welcomed as manager of the saloon and gambling house owned by the Denver firm of Watrous, Banniger, and Company. Bat worked the floor sixteen hours daily. Though a short man who often wore a corduroy suit of lavendar offset by a plain black tie, all knew Bat by reputation. The cry, "Here comes Masterson!" was usually all that was necessary to calm any disorderly customer.

Another of Bat's duties in Creede was serving as referee when Billy Woods, self-proclaimed heavyweight champion of Colorado, fought. Woods managed the Denver Exchange in addition to his boxing activities. Bat may have been somewhat partial to his employer Woods, but was evidently knowledgeable about boxing. Bat had been a second to Jake Kilrain when Kilrain lost the heavyweight championship to John L. Sullivan July 8, 1889, at Richburg, Mississippi, in the historic seventy-five round battle which marked the end of bare knuckles championships.

Though Creede began fairly quietly for a boom town it grew more lively with the passing days. As early as February 25, 1893, Bat had felt the town's capability for violence when he was interviewed by a Denver reporter writing for the **Sun.** The reporter described Bat as, "one of the terrors of the West . . . of muscular build and pleasant face. He is quiet in demeanor and sober in habit. There is no blow or bluff or bullyism about him. He attends strictly to business. He has been known to take a slap in

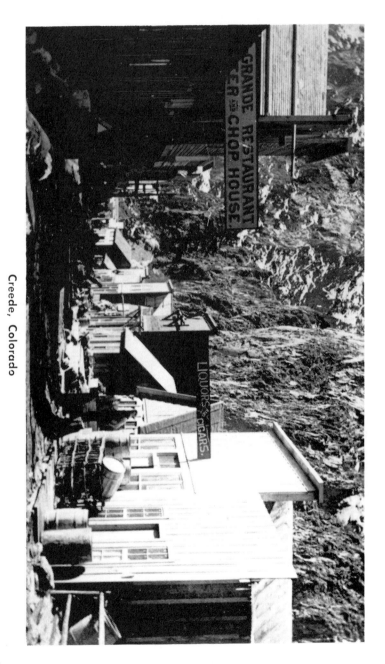

Creede, Colorado

State Historical Society of Colorado Library

the face from some drunken fool who didn't know his record, and not resent the insult . . . He is here in the interest of peace, having a commission from certain Denver parties to maintain order in their gambling places."

During that same interview Bat proclaimed, " I don't like this quiet. It augurs ill. I have been in several places that started out this way and there were generaly wild scenes of carnage before many weeks passed." In this Bat proved prophetic.

Creede soon boasted a "Shotgun Graveyard" where space was reserved for those who died of gunshot wounds. Rascals and cutthroats of all types were drawn to the magnet called Creede. Bob Ford, who claimed fame as the killer of Jesse James, let it be known Creede was his town. A short while later Jefferson Randolph "Soapy" Smith arrived and allowed otherwise. Creede, said Smith, was his town. Ford decided part of a town was better than all of a grave and agreed.

As was the custom of the day both Bat and Soapy on occasion wore the badge of town marshal though neither was active in law enforcement. Bat cared little for Soapy so long as he was allowed to run his business in a profitable manner. Soapy doubtless felt somewhat the same so the pair got along even to the point of playing poker at the same table.

Cigar smoking Poker Alice Tubbs often sat in on Bat's games in Creede. Another one-time poker player was Ed O. Kelly. In the course of one game Kelly incurred the wrath of Bat who suggested quite firmly that Kelly leave Creede. Soapy, who was also in the game, took the stance of observer and watched. Kelly chose to ignore Bat's good advice. A short time after the disputed poker game Kelly took a shotgun to Bob Ford and became "the man who shot the man who shot Jesse James." Instead of instant recognition Ed O. Kelly drew a prison sentence, perhaps proving he should have heeded Bat's advice.

When the Creede boom showed signs of an early slowing, Bat returned to Denver. Eventually he found his way into fight promotion, possibly in an effort to keep the boxing game reasonably honest despite the manipulations and showmanship of Soapy Smith whose return to Denver closely paralleled Bat's. Soapy went in for such nonsense as fighters in wooden clogs

"Poker Alice" Tubbs

Denver Public Library, Western History Department

Jefferson Randolph "Soapy" Smith

Denver Public Library, Western History Department

and the like. Bat favored fighters who fought. Bat's ideas won out or perhaps the lure of boom town won out. Soapy harkened to the call of the Klondike while Bat remained in Denver on the sporting scene. Even the fact that Wyatt Earp was running a saloon-gambling hall in Nome seemed not to appeal to Bat. He had "hung up his guns" in favor of the boxing scene. Of course old gunmen never totally leave the trade as witnessed to by the fact Bat was in charge of the special police at the Corbett-Fitzsimmons fight in Carson City, Nevada, on March 17, 1897.

Three weeks before the Corbett fight Bat had become involved in a bribery scandal which involved members of the state legislature. On February 25, 1897, the **Rocky Mountain News** printed the story which concerned the El Paso County division bill. As a result of the disclosures Bat was called before a Senate committee that night but never appeared to testify. He left town either the evening of the 25th or early the 26th and was not to be found.

Bat had claimed certain Colorado Springs persons requested him to lobby against county division and after he had, refused to pay him. Bat had no written or verbal agreement that he be paid a specific sum. "All he had was assurance that they would do right by him."

When Bat was not paid he threatened exposure which he followed through on. Bat gave the story to T. M. Patterson whose editorial told Bat's side. Patterson was subpoenaed by the committee and answered questions about the story. Numerous other witnesses were called, all of whom knew Bat, but little about the bribery. No major decision was reached after the committee gathered testimony and when Bat again returned to Denver nothing further was said concerning the affair.

By April 9, 1899, the Colorado Athletic Association was founded. Bat was listed as official referee and ponderous Otto C. Floto, **Denver Post's** sports editor, was vice-president. A month later **Post** publishers Harry H. Tammen and Frederick G. Bonfils supported Floto in a move which froze out the other members of the CAA, Bat among them.

Bat, not one to back away from a fight, at once organized the Olympic Athletic Club with himself as president. He leased the old Academy of Music at Sixteen and Market and began to offer Floto competition. Fighting was illegal at the time but injunctions keeping the Denver Fire and Police Commission from interfering were easily obtained. The commissioners themselves enjoyed the boxing game.

The Olympic's brief history became one of alternating success and setbacks. Newspapers announced that the club's first bout would be held May 20, 1899. On May 16, Bat was denied permission to hold the fight. However, by July 11, it was reported that Bat had secured an injunction restraining the fire and police board from interfering in fights at the Olympic Athletic Club. It can be assumed this injunction was permanent as no further mention of cancellation is to be found and a month later the **Times** was calling Bat the "Dignified Sheik of the Olympic Athletic Club."

Bat acted as referee for the Olympic's main events, a job which often involved keeping the fans in check as much as the fighters. At the Rublin-Lawler match on July 28, 1899, the fans howled for Lawler's blood following a series of deliberate fouls. Bat reasoned with the crowd saying, "You fellows came here to see a fight, didn't you? Well, let these fellows fight. They will get down to fair fighting after a bit." They did. Rublin won by a KO in the ninth.

The Cannon Prize Fight Bill legalized boxing in Colorado but Bat was broke. The summer of 1900 the Olympic became a lodging house. President-to-be Theodore Roosevelt whom Bat had met on one of Roosevelt's Western jaunts, offered Bat the post of United States Marshal in Oklahoma. Bat declined, saying he had "taken his guns off" and could see no good coming from accepting the post.

One July evening Bat followed "huge, balloon-shaped" Floto from the **Post** building to a cafe at Sixteenth and Champa. The hulking Floto symbolized all that was wrong in Bat's life. The **Times** reported that Bat put his gold-headed cane to good use that evening. Floto thought it best to run before the wrath of the cane-wielding smaller man. Bat told the **Times** Floto was the best runner he had ever seen. He further said some fellows had to be beaten to death to be taught to be decent. Masterson further understood Floto carried a derringer. Bat let it be known he intended to relieve Floto of the weapon and pawn it for five dollars.

The fact that Bat had let his temper get the better of him was indicative of his general condition. Denver, termed by author Peter Lyon as "then notoriously the crookedest town in the country" had lost the charm it once held for Bat. During an interview in the **Times** in September, 1900, Bat had nothing to say in favor of the Queen City of the Plains.

Otto Floto

Denver Public Library, Western History Department

Bat told the reporter, "This town is the worst in the country and the worst in the state. This place is the butt of the country. It is a great hospital in which are gathered more old, broken-down fossils, fakirs, and bunks than can be gathered up with a fine comb by dragging it through the whole country."

Small wonder that Bat sent his wife to Philadelphia with the promise he would be joining her soon.

Added to Bat's own personal feelings was the fact that **Post** owners Bonfils and Tammens were not happy at the picture of their sports editor scurrying down the street like a kicked pup. Then Bat appeared wearing his .45. Denver's police chief and district attorney, with perhaps a bit of prompting from the offended newspapermen, decided they were fearful of the consequences. They called in Cripple Creek's city marshal, a gun slinger named Jim Marshall. Bat was tipped and wired Marshall to meet him at the barbershop in the rear of Scholtz drugstore. Marshall did not show.

Bat waited a reasonable time before leaving to get a drink at a nearby bar. Hardly had Bat established himself at the bar when cold steel was pressed into his back. Bat and Jim discussed Bat's position. Bat agreed to be on the 4:00 Burlington and Jim holstered his weapon. The aging Bat packed, and boarded the train. His Colorado career was at an end.

President Roosevelt befriended Bat in the East. Eventually Bat became sports editor for the New York **Morning Telegraph,** the job he still held when he died at his desk the morning of October 25, 1921.

January 13, 1929, Wyatt Earp died in Los Angeles, and an era in Western history was at an end.

BIBLIOGRAPHY

BOOKS

——————, *History of the Arkansas Valley, Colorado,* Chicago, Illinois: O. L. Baskin & Co., Historical Publishers. 1881.

Jahns, Pat, *The Frontier World of Doc Holliday: Faro Dealer from Dallas to Deadwood.* New York, New York: Hastings House Publishers, 1957.

Lake, Stuart N., *Wyatt Earp, Frontier Marshal.* Boston, Massachusetts: Houghton Mifflin Company, 1931.

Marshall, James, *Santa Fe: The Railroad That Built An Empire.* New York, New York: Random House, 1945.

Mumey, Nolie, *Creede: History of a Colorado Mining Town.* Denver, Colorado: Artcraft Press, 1949.

Myers, John Myers, *Doc Holliday.* Boston, Massachusetts: Little, Brown and Company. 1955.

O'Connor, Richard, *Bat Masterson.* Garden City, New York: Doubleday & Company, Inc., 1957.

Parkhill, Forbes, *The Wildest of the West.* New York, New York: Henry Holt and Company, 1951.

Robertson, Frank G., and Harris, Beth Kay, *Soapy Smith: King of the Frontier Con Men.* New York, New York: Hastings House Publishers, 1961.

Wallace, Betty, *Gunnison County.* Denver, Colorado: Sage Books, 1960.

PERIODICALS

Lyon, Peter. "The Wild, Wild West, *American Heritage* (New York, New York) Vol. XI, No. 5, (August, 1960), 32-48.

NEWSPAPERS

The Colorado Sun
Denver *Republican*
Denver *Times*
Denver *Tribune-Republican*
Gunnison *Daily News Democrat*
Gunnison *News-Champion*
Pueblo *Chieftain*
Rocky Mountain News

INDEX